The ESSENTIALS of

Macroeconomics I

Robert S. Rycroft, Ph.D.
Chairperson of Economics Department
Mary Washington College, Fredericksburg, VA

Research & Education Association
Visit our website at
www.rea.com

Research & Education Association
61 Ethel Road West
Piscataway, New Jersey 08854
E-mail: info@rea.com

THE ESSENTIALS®
OF MACROECONOMICS I

Year 2006 Printing

Printed in the United States of America

Library of Congress Control Number 99-74564

International Standard Book Number 0-87891-700-4

What REA's Essentials®
Will Do for You

This book is part of REA's celebrated *Essentials*® series of review and study guides, relied on by tens of thousands of students over the years for being complete yet concise.

Here you'll find a summary of the very material you're most likely to need for exams, not to mention homework—eliminating the need to read and review many pages of textbook and class notes.

This slim volume condenses the vast amount of detail characteristic of the subject matter and summarizes the **essentials** of the field. The book provides quick access to the important facts, principles, theorems, concepts, and equations of the field.

It will save you hours of study and preparation time.

This *Essentials*® book has been prepared by experts in the field and has been carefully reviewed to ensure its accuracy and maximum usefulness. We believe you'll find it a valuable, handy addition to your library.

Larry B. Kling
Chief Editor

CONTENTS

CHAPTER 1

INTRODUCTION TO ECONOMICS

1.1 WHAT IS ECONOMICS?

Economics—"Economics is what economists do." This statement, attributed to the famous economist Jacob Viner, may in fact be the best description of the discipline available. What it says is that economics cannot be defined by a series of topics that all economists study. For example, contrary to widespread belief, economics is **not** the study of business. Topics in business certainly occupy the time of many economists, but there is much more to it. It is more accurate to say that economics is a particular way of looking at topics. **It is a methodology for analyzing situations where human beings have to make choices from limited options.** Consequently, it can be used to study such business-related issues as capital investment, pricing policy, and interest rates, but it can also be used to look at the "bigger" issues of inflation, unemployment, economic growth, and the "non-economic" issues of love, marriage, child-bearing, and discrimination, to name but a few.

1

Macroeconomics—Macroeconomics is the study of the economy as a whole. Some of the topics considered include inflation, unemployment, and economic growth.

Microeconomics—Microeconomics is the study of the individual parts that make up the economy. The parts include households, business firms, and government agencies. Particular emphasis is placed on how these units make decisions and the consequences of these decisions.

1.2 ECONOMIC ANALYSIS

Economic Theory—An economic theory is an explanation of why certain economic phenomena occur. For example, there are theories explaining the rate of inflation, how many hours people choose to work, and the amount of goods and services the U.S. will import. Stripped down to essentials, a theory is a set of statements about cause and effect relationships in the economy.

Models—A model is an abstract replica of reality, and is the formal statement of a theory. The best models retain the essence of the reality, but do away with extraneous details. Virtually all economic analysis is done by first constructing a model of the situation the economist wants to analyze. The reason for this is because human beings are incapable of fully understanding reality. It is too complex for the human mind. Models, because they avoid many of the messier details of reality, can be comprehended, but good models are always "unrealistic."

It would not be inaccurate to say that economists do not analyze the economy, they analyze models of the economy. Almost every prediction that an economist makes, e.g., the impact of changes in the money supply on interest rates, the effect

2

of the unemployment rate on the rate of inflation, the effect of increased competition in an industry on profits, is based on a model.

Models come in verbal, graphical, or mathematical form.

Empirical Analysis—All models yield predictions about the economy. For example, a widely-held model predicts that increases in the rate of growth of the money supply will lead to higher inflation. In empirical analysis, economists compare predictions with the actual performance of the economy as measured by economic data. Good empirical analysis often requires mastery of sophisticated statistical and mathematical tools.

Positive Economics—Positive economics is the analysis of "what if." For example, positive economics tries to answer such questions as these: What will the effect be on the rate of inflation if the rate of growth of the money supply is raised by one percentage point? What will happen to hours of work of welfare recipients if welfare benefits are raised $500? What will the effect be on our trade balance if the exchange rate is devalued 5%? Many economists view positive economics as "objective" or "scientific," and believe their special training gives them the expertise to draw conclusions about these types of issues.

Normative Economics—Normative economics is the analysis of "what should be." For example, normative economics tries to answer such questions as these: What inflation rate should our economy strive for? Should welfare recipients be expected to work? Is reducing our trade deficit a desirable thing? Normative economics is clearly a subjective area. There is nothing in an economist's training that gives his or her opinions on these issues any more validity than anyone else's.

1.3   THE ECONOMIC WAY OF THINKING

Economics analysis is characterized by an emphasis on certain fundamental concepts.

Scarcity—Human wants and needs (for goods, services, leisure, etc.) exceed the ability of the economy to satisfy those wants and needs. This is true for the economy as a whole as well as each individual in the economy. In other words, there is never enough to go around. Individuals never have enough money to buy all they want. Business firms cannot pay completely satisfactory wages without cutting into profits, and vice-versa. Government never has enough money to fund all worthwhile projects. The concept of scarcity is discussed again in Section 2.1.

Opportunity Cost—The reality of scarcity implies that individuals, businesses, and governments must make choices, selecting some opportunities while foregoing others. Buying a car may mean foregoing a vacation; acquiring a new copy machine may mean cancelling the company picnic; paying higher welfare benefits may require terminating a weapons system. The opportunity cost of a choice is the value of the best alternative choice sacrificed.

Individualism—Economic analysis emphasizes individual action. Most economic theories attempt to model the behavior of "typical" individuals. All groups, such as "society," business firms, or unions, are analyzed as a collection of individuals each acting in a particular way. In a sense, the preceding sentence represents an ideal. Not all economic theory achieves this goal.

Rational Behavior—Individuals are assumed to act rationally. This is the most misunderstood term in economics. It does not necessarily mean people are cold, calculating, and greedy. Rather, it means that given a person's goals and knowledge, people take actions likely to achieve those goals and avoid actions likely to detract from those goals. A greedy person acts rationally if she spends on herself and does not give to charity. She is irrational if she does the opposite. An altruistic person acts rationally if she gives her money to the needy and does not spend on herself. Irrational behavior is the opposite.

Marginal Analysis—Economists assume that people make choices by weighing the costs and benefits of particular actions.

1.4   IMPORTANT ECONOMIC CONCEPTS AND TERMS (NOT ELSEWHERE DEFINED)

Specialization and Division of Labor—This is a strategy for producing goods and services. Division of labor means that different members of a team of producers are given responsibility for different aspects of a production plan. Specialization means that producers become quite apt at those aspects of production they concentrate on. Specialization and division of labor is alleged to lead to efficiency which facilitates economic growth and development.

CHAPTER 2

THE ECONOMIC PROBLEM

2.1 UNIVERSALITY OF THE PROBLEM OF SCARCITY

Goods and Services—Goods and Services refers to anything that satisfies human needs, wants, or desires. Goods are tangible items, such as food, cars, and clothing. Services are intangible items such as education, health care, and leisure. The consumption of goods and services is a source of happiness, well-being, satisfaction, or utility.

Resources (Factors of Production)—Resources refers to anything that can be used to produce goods and services. A commonly-used classification scheme places all resources into one of five categories:

Land—All natural resources, whether on the land, under the land, in the water, or in the air; e.g., fertile agricultural land, iron ore deposits, tuna fish, corn seeds, and quail.

Labor—The work effort of human beings.

Capital—Productive implements made by human beings; e.g., factories, machinery, and tools.

Entrepreneurship—A specialized form of labor. Entrepreneurship is creative labor. It refers to the ability to detect new business opportunities and bring them to fruition. Entrepreneurs also manage the other factors of production.

Technology—The practical application of scientific knowledge. Technology is typically combined with the other factors to make them more productive.

Scarcity—Economists assume that human wants and needs are virtually limitless while acknowledging that the resources to satisfy those needs are limited. Consequently, society is never able to produce enough goods and services to satisfy everybody, or most anyone, completely. Alternatively, resources are scarce relative to human needs and desires.

Scarcity is a problem of all societies, whether rich or poor. As a mental experiment, write down the amount of income you think a typical family needs to be "comfortable" in the United States today: _____ Now compare your figure with the median family income in the United States found on page 41. In most instances, what students think is necessary to be comfortable far exceeds median family income, which loosely implies that the typical family in the U.S. is not comfortable, even though we are the richest nation in the history of the world. If your figure is less than median income, think again. Do you think you would really be "comfortable" at that level of income?

2.2 UNIVERSAL PROBLEMS CAUSED BY SCARCITY

A society without scarcity is a society without problems, and, consequently, one where there is no need to make decisions. In the real world, all societies must make three crucial decisions:

1. **What goods and services to produce and in what quantities.**

2. **How to produce the goods and services selected —** what resource combinations and production techniques to use.

3. **How to distribute the goods and services produced among people —** who gets how much of each good and service produced.

2.3 UNIVERSAL ECONOMIC GOALS

Allocative (Economic) Efficiency—A society achieves allocative efficiency if it produces the types and quantities of goods and services that most satisfy its people. Failure to do so wastes resources.

Technical Efficiency—A society achieves technical efficiency when it is producing the greatest quantity of goods and services possible from its resources. Failure to do so is also a waste of resources.

Equity—A society wants the distribution of goods and services to conform with its notions of "fairness."

Standards of Equity—Equity is not necessarily synonymous with equality. There is no objective standard of equity, and all societies have different notions of what constitutes equity. Three widely-held standards are:

1. **Contributory standard**—Under a contributory standard, people are entitled to a share of goods and services based on what they contribute to society. Those making larger contributions receive correspondingly larger shares. The measurement of contribution and what to do about those who contribute very little or are unable to contribute (i.e., the disabled) are continuing issues.

2. **Needs standard**—Under a needs standard, a person's contribution to society is irrelevant. Goods and services are distributed based on the needs of different households. Measuring need and inducing people to contribute to society when goods and services are guaranteed are continuing issues.

3. **Equality Standard**—Under an equality standard, every person is entitled to an equal share of goods and services, simply because he or she is a human being. Allowing for needs and inducing people to make maximum productive efforts when the reward is the same for all are continuing issues.

Economists remain divided over whether the goals of equity and efficiency (allocative and technical) are complementary or in conflict.

2.4 PRODUCTION POSSIBILITIES CURVE

The Production Possibilities Curve is a model of the economy used to illustrate the problems associated with scarcity. It shows the maximum feasible combinations of two goods or services that society can produce, assuming all resources are used in their most productive manner.

ASSUMPTIONS OF THE MODEL

1. Society is only capable of producing two goods (Guns and Butter).

2. At a given point in time, society has a fixed quantity of resources.

3. All resources are used in their most productive manner.

Table 2.1 shows selected combinations of the two goods that can be produced given the assumptions.

Point	Guns	Butter
A	0	16
B	4	14
C	7	12
D	9	9
E	10	5
F	11	0

TABLE 2.1–Selected Combinations of Guns and Butter

Figure 2.1 is a graphical depiction of the production possibilities curve (curve FA).

Technical Efficiency—All points on the curve are points of technical efficiency. By definition, technical efficiency is achieved when more of one good cannot be produced without producing less of the other good. Find point D on the curve. Any move to a point with more guns (i.e., point E) will necessitate a reduction in butter production. Any move to a point

10

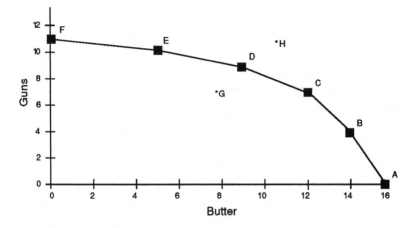

FIGURE 2.1–Production Possibilities Curve

with more butter (such as point C) will necessitate a reduction in guns production. Any point inside the curve (such as point G) represents technical inefficiency. Either inefficient production methods are being used or resources are not fully employed. A movement from G to the curve will allow more of one or both goods to be produced without any reduction in the quantity of the other good. Points outside the curve (such as H) are technically infeasible given society's current stock of resources and technological knowledge.

Opportunity Cost—Consider a move from D to E. Society gets one more unit of guns, but must sacrifice 4 units of butter. The 4 units of butter is the opportunity cost of the gun. One gun costs 4 butter.

Law of Increasing Costs—Starting from point A and moving up along the curve, note that the opportunity cost of guns increases. From point A to B, 2 butter are sacrificed to get 4 guns (1 gun costs $\frac{1}{2}$ butter); from point B to C, 2 butter are sacrificed to get 3 guns (1 gun costs $\frac{2}{3}$ butter); from C to D, 3 butter are sacrificed for 2 guns (1 gun costs 1-$\frac{1}{2}$ butter); from

11

D to E, 1 gun costs 4 butter; from E to F, 1 gun costs 5 butter.

The law of increasing costs says that as more of a good or service is produced, its opportunity cost will rise. It is a consequence of resources being specialized in particular uses. Some resources are particularly good in gun production and not so good for butter production, and vice-versa.

At the commencement of gun production, the resources shifted out of butter will be those least productive in butter (and most productive in guns). Consequently, gun production will rise with little cost in terms of butter. As more resources are diverted, those more productive in butter will be affected, and the opportunity cost will rise. This is what gives the production possibilities curve its characteristic convex shape.

If resources are not specialized in particular uses, opportunity costs will remain constant and the production possibilities curve will be a straight line (see Figure 2.2).

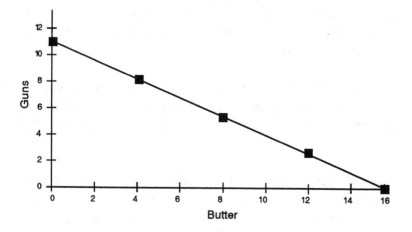

**FIGURE 2.2–Production Possibilities Curve
When Resources Not Specialized**

Allocative Efficiency—Allocative efficiency will be represented by the point on the curve that best satisfies society's needs and wants. It cannot be located without additional knowledge of society's likes and dislikes. A complicating factor is that the allocatively efficient point is not independent of society's distribution of income and wealth.

Economic Growth—Society's production of goods and services is limited by its resources. Economic growth, then, requires that society increase the amount of resources it has or makes those resources more productive through the application of technology. Graphically, economic growth is represented by an outward shift of the curve to IJ (see Table 2.3). Economic growth will make more combinations of goods and services feasible, but will not end the problem of scarcity.

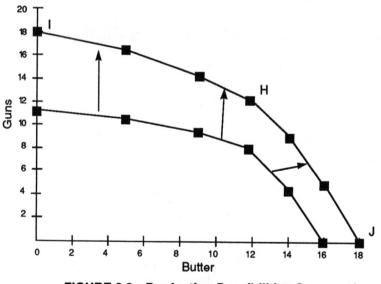

FIGURE 2.3—Production Possibilities Curve and Economic Growth

13

CHAPTER 3

DEMAND AND SUPPLY

3.1 DEMAND

Demand—Demand is a schedule or a graph showing the relationship between the price of a product and the amount consumers are willing and able to buy, ceteris paribus. The schedule or graph does not necessarily show what consumers actually buy at each price. The Law of Demand says there is an inverse relationship between price and quantity demanded, people will be willing and able to buy more if the product gets cheaper.

CETERIS PARIBUS

All hypothetical relationships between variables in economics include a stated or implied assumption ceteris paribus. The term means "all other factors held constant." As we will see, there are many factors affecting the amount of a product people are willing and able to buy. The demand schedule shows the relationship between price and quantity demanded, holding all the other factors constant. This allows us to investigate the independent effect that price changes have on quantity demanded without worrying about the influence the other factors are having.

Demand Schedule–Assume the product is widgets. Let Qd be quantity demanded and P be price.

Qd	P
48.0	1.00
47.5	1.25
47.0	1.50
46.5	1.75
46.0	2.00

Demand Graph–See Figure 3.1.

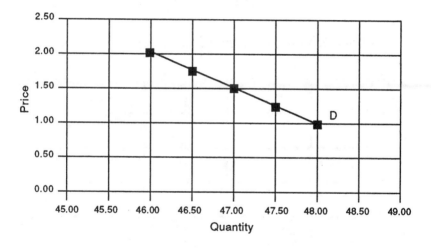

FIGURE 3.1–Graph of Demand Schedule

3.2 SUPPLY

Supply—Supply is a schedule or a graph showing the relationship between the price of a product and the amount producers are willing and able to supply, ceteris paribus. The schedule or graph does not necessarily show what producers actually sell at each price. There is generally a positive relationship between price and quantity supplied, reflecting higher costs associated with greater production.

Supply Schedule–Assume the product is widgets. Let Qs be quantity supplied.

Qs	P
46.0	1.00
46.5	1.25
47.0	1.50
47.5	1.75
48.0	2.00

Supply Graph—See Figure 3.2.

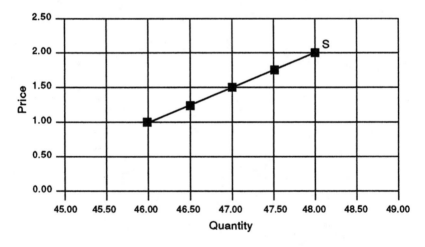

FIGURE 3.2–Graph of Supply Schedule

3.3 MARKET EQUILIBRIUM

The intersection of the demand and supply curves indicate the equilibrium price and quantity in the market (see Figure

3.3). The word equilibrium is synonymous with stable. The price and quantity in a market will frequently not be equal to the equilibrium, but if that is the case then the market will be adjusting, and, hence, not stable.

If the price of the product is $2.00, then the quantity supplied of the product (48) will be greater than the quantity demanded (46). There will be a surplus in the market of 48 – 46 = 2. The unsold product will force producers to lower their prices. A reduction in price will reduce the quantity supplied while increasing quantity demanded until the surplus disappears. Two dollars is not an equilibrium because the market is forced to adjust.

If the price of the product is $1.00, then the quantity supplied of the product (46) will be less than the quantity demanded (48). There will be a shortage in the market of 48 – 46 = 2. Unsatisfied customers will cause the price of the product to be bid up. The higher price will cause the quantity supplied to increase while decreasing the quantity demanded until the

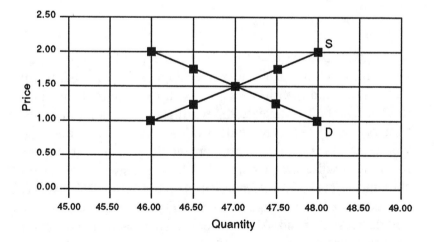

FIGURE 3.3–Market Equilibrium

17

shortage disappears. One dollar is not an equilibrium because the market is forced to adjust.

If the price of the product is $1.50, then the quantity demanded (47) is just equal to the quantity supplied (47). Producers can sell all they want. Buyers can buy all they want. Since everyone is satisfied, there is no reason for the price to change. Hence, $1.50 is an equilibrium price and 47 is an equilibrium quantity.

3.4   SHIFTS IN DEMAND

Price is not the only factor affecting the amount consumers are willing and able to buy. Other factors include:

1. Consumer tastes

2. Income

3. Prices of other goods

4. Price expectations

Graphically, the effect of these factors can be represented by shifts in the demand curve (see Figure 3.4). A rightward/outward/upward shift in the curve is an increase in demand (D to D'). Events that increase the willingness and ability of consumers to buy will increase demand. Alternatively, events that would increase the price consumers would be willing to pay for the product will increase demand. A leftward/inward/downward shift in the curve is a decrease in demand (D to D''). Events that decrease the willingness and ability of consumers to buy will decrease demand. Alternatively, events that would decrease the price that consumers would pay for a good would decrease demand.

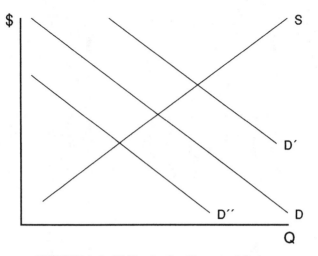

FIGURE 3.4–Shifts in the Demand Curve

Normal Good or Service—A good or service that consumers want to buy more of when their income rises, e.g., filet mignon.

Inferior Good or Service—A good or service that consumers want to buy less of when their income rises, e.g., margarine.

Substitute Good or Service—A good or service that can be used in place of another good or service, e.g., wheat bread and white bread.

Complement Good or Service—A good or service whose use increases the enjoyment a consumer gets from another good or service, e.g., bread and butter—butter makes bread taste better.

Change in Demand vs. Change in Quantity Demanded—Factors that shift the demand curve cause changes in demand. These are changes in income, tastes, prices of other goods, and price expectations. Note that changes in the price of the prod-

Factor	Event	Shift Demand Curve	Equilibrium Price	Equilibrium Quantity
Tastes	Consumers prefer product more	out	increase	increase
	Consumers prefer product less	in	decrease	decrease
Income	Normal good — income increases	out	increase	increase
	Normal good — income decreases	in	decrease	decrease
	Inferior good — income increases	in	decrease	decrease
	Inferior good — income decreases	out	increase	increase
Price of Related Goods	Substitute good — price increases	out	increase	increase
	Substitute good — price decreases	in	decrease	decrease
	Complement good – price increases	in	decrease	decrease
	Complement good — price decreases	out	increase	increase
Price Expectations	Price level expected to rise	out	increase	increase
	Price level expected to fall	in	decrease	decrease

TABLE 3.1–Shifts in the Demand Curve

uct is not included on this list. A movement from one point to another along an existing demand curve represents a change in quantity demanded. This can only result from a change in the price of the product.

3.5 SHIFTS IN SUPPLY

Price is not the only factor affecting the amount producers are willing and able to supply. Other factors include:

1. Costs of resources

2. Changes in technology

3. Unexpected events

4. Price expectations

5. Direct taxes on the product

Graphically, the effect of these factors can be represented by shifts in the supply curve (see Figure 3.5). A rightward/outward/downward shift in the curve is an increase in supply (S to S'). Events that would increase the willingness and ability of firms to supply output would increase supply. Alternatively, events that would lower the cost of producing any level of output would increase supply. A leftward/inward/upward shift in the curve is a decrease in supply (S to S''). Events that would decrease the willingness and ability of firms to supply output would decrease supply. Alternatively, events that would raise the cost of producing output would decrease supply.

Change in Supply vs. Change in Quantity Supplied— Factors that shift the supply curve cause changes in supply. These are changes in cost of resources, technology, unexpected

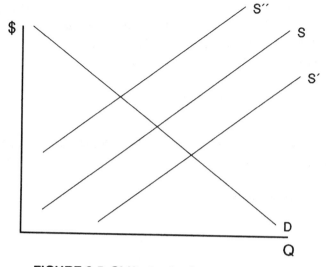

FIGURE 3.5–Shifts in the Supply Curve

events, price expectations and direct taxes. Note that the price of the product is not included on this list. A movement from one point to another along an existing supply curve represents a change in supply. This can only result from a change in the price of the product.

3.6 PRICE CONTROLS

An equilibrium price is not necessarily a "fair" price. It could happen that the equilibrium price in a market is higher than society considers "fair." It could also happen that an equilibrium price in a market is lower than society considers "fair." There has been a long history of governments imposing price controls in markets where prices are considered a "problem."

Price Ceiling—A price ceiling is a government mandated level above which a price cannot go. Price ceilings are frequently set where equilibrium prices promise to be "too high." An example would be rent controls in cities. An often unappre-

Factor	Event	Shift Supply Curve	Equilibrium Price	Equilibrium Quantity
Costs of Resources	Resource costs increase	in	increase	decrease
	Resource costs decrease	out	decrease	increase
Technology	Technology advances	out	decrease	increase
	Technology retreats	in	increase	decrease
Unexpected Events	Product destruction	in	increase	decrease
Price Expectations	Product price expected to rise	in	increase	decrease
	Product price expected to fall	out	decrease	increase
Taxes	direct taxes on product rise	in	increase→	decrease→
	direct taxes on product fall	out	decrease→	increase→

TABLE 3.2–Shifts in the Supply Curve

23

ciated side-effect of a price ceiling is to create an artificial shortage of the product and to lead to black markets in the product.

In the market (see Figure 3.6) the equilibrium price is $1.50 and equilibrium quantity is 47. If government imposes a price ceiling preventing prices from rising above $1.00, producers will reduce quantity supplied to 46 while consumers will increase their quantity demanded to 48. A shortage of 48 – 46 = 2 will result.

Price Floor—A price floor is a government mandated level below which a price cannot go. Price floors are frequently set where equilibrium prices promise to be "too low." An example would be the minimum wage. An often unappreciated side-effect of a price floor is to create an artificial surplus (e.g., unemployment) of the item and to lead to black markets.

In the market, the equilibrium price is $1.50 and equilibrium quantity is 47. If government imposes a price floor preventing prices from falling below $2.00, producers will increase their quantity supplied to 48 while consumers reduce their quantity demanded to 46. A surplus of 48 – 46 = 2 will result.

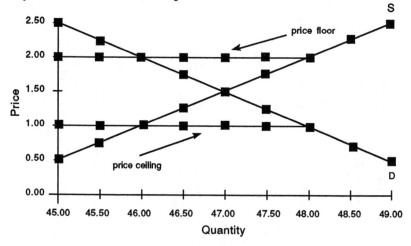

FIGURE 3.6–Price Controls

CHAPTER 4

ECONOMIC SYSTEMS

4.1 TYPES OF SYSTEMS

Every society must have some method for making the basic economic decisions defined in 2.2.

Tradition—Traditional systems largely rely on custom to determine production and distribution questions. While not static, traditional systems are slow to change and are not well-equipped to propel a society into sustained growth. Traditional systems are found in many of the poorer Third World countries.

Command—Command economies rely on a central authority to make decisions. The central authority may be a dictator or a democratically constituted government.

Market—It is easier to describe what a market system is not than what it is. In a pure market system, there is no central authority and custom plays very little role. Every consumer makes buying decisions based on his or her own needs and desires and income. Individual self-interest rules. Every producer decides for him- or herself what goods or services to produce, what price to charge, what resources to employ, and what production methods to use. Producers are motivated solely by profit considerations. There is vigorous competition in every market.

Mixed—A mixed economy contains elements of each of the three systems defined above. All real world economies are mixed economies, although the mixture of tradition, command, and market differs greatly. The U.S. economy has traditionally placed great emphasis on the market, although there is a large and active government (command) sector. The Soviet economy places main reliance on government to direct economic activity, but there is a small market sector.

Capitalism—The key characteristic of a capitalistic economy is that productive resources are owned by private individuals.

Socialism—The key characteristic of a socialist economy is that productive resources are owned collectively by society. Alternatively, productive resources are under the control of government.

4.2 CIRCULAR FLOW

The Circular Flow is a model of economic relationships in a capitalistic market economy. Households, the owners of all productive resources, supply resources to firms through the resource markets, receiving monetary payments in return. Firms use the resources purchased (or rented, as the case may be) to produce goods and services, which are then sold to households and other businesses in the product markets. Household income not spent (consumed) may be saved in the Financial Markets. Firms may borrow from the financial markets to finance capital

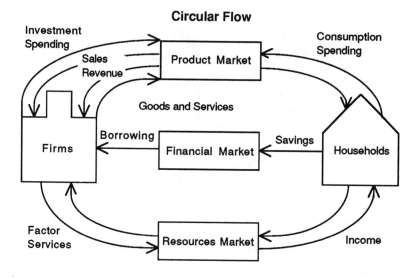

FIGURE 4.1–The Circular Flow

expansion (investment). Firm saving and household borrowing
are not shown.

4.3   HOW A MARKET ECONOMY WORKS

Although the description of a market economy may suggest
that chaos is the order of the day, economists believe that if
certain conditions are met (see Section 4.4) a market economy
is easily capable of achieving the major economic goals.

**How a Market Economy Achieves Allocation Effi-
ciency**—Market forces will lead firms to produce the mix of
goods most desired. Unforeseen events can be responded to in
a rational manner.

4.3.1   CHANGE IN TASTES

Assume a change in consumer tastes from beef to chicken

(see Figure 4.2). An increase in demand in the chicken market will be accompanied by a decrease in demand in the beef market. The higher price of chicken will attract more resources into the market and lead to an increase in the quantity supplied. The lower price of beef will induce a reduction in the quantity supplied and exit of resources to other industries.

Change in Tastes

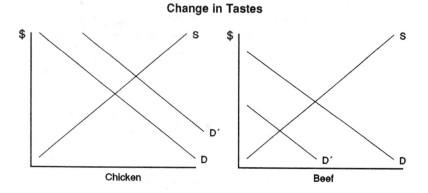

FIGURE 4.2–Change in Tastes

Note that the change in the level of output of both goods occurred because it was in the economic self-interest of firms to do so. Greater demand in the chicken market increased the profitability of chicken; lower demand in the beef market decreased the profitability of beef. Chicken and beef producers responded to society's desires not out of a sense of public spiritedness, but out of self-interest.

4.3.2 SCARCITY

An unexpected freeze in Florida will shift in the supply curve of orange juice, driving up its price, and causing consumers to cut back their purchases (see Figure 4.3). The higher price of orange juice will increase the demand for substitute products like apple juice, causing an increase in the quantity supplied of apple juice to take the place of orange juice.

28

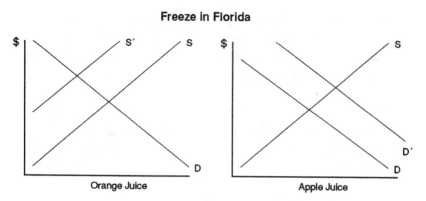

Freeze in Florida

Orange Juice

Apple Juice

FIGURE 4.3–Freeze in Florida

As above, the reaction of market participants reflected their evaluation of their own self-interest. Consumers reduced their quantity demanded of orange juice because it was now more expensive. Apple juice producers expanded production because now it was more profitable.

Consumer Sovereignty—"The Consumer is King." Consumer sovereignty means that consumers determine what is produced in the economy. In a market economy, business must cater to the whims of consumer tastes or else go out of business.

How a Market Economy Achieves Technical Efficiency—Market forces will lead firms to produce output in the most efficient manner. The constant struggle for profits will stimulate firms to cut costs. Note that technical efficiency results from attention to self-interest, not the public interest.

The Importance of Competition—A market economy thrives on competition between firms. In their struggle for survival, firms will be forced to cater to consumer demand (leading to allocative efficiency) and force production costs down as far as possible (leading to technical efficiency).

29

How a Market Economy Achieves Full Employment—Full employment of resources is thought to be the normal state of affairs in a market economy. Resource surpluses will force down the resource's price, leading quickly to re-employment.

How a Market Economy Achieves Growth—Competition between firms for the consumer's dollar will force a constant search for better products and methods of production. The resulting technological change will lead to optimal growth.

The Market Economy and Equity—This is a problematic area for a market economy. Certainly there are financial rewards for those who produce the products that win consumer acceptance. There are losses for those who do not. Yet winners in a market economy are not necessarily the most virtuous of people, they just sell a better product. While consumer demand determines the pattern of production, those consumers with the most income exert the greatest influence on the pattern.

The Role of Prices in a Market Economy—In order for an economy to operate efficiently, there must be **information** and **incentives**. There must be information on what goods and services are in demand, which resources are scarce, and so on. There must be an incentive to produce the goods and services desired, conserve on scarce resources, and so on. Both information and incentives are provided by prices. High prices indicate goods and services in demand; low prices indicate goods and services that have lost favor. High prices indicate scarce resources; low prices indicate plentiful. Firms responding "properly" to high prices will earn profits; firms responding "properly" to low prices will avoid losses. Firms exploiting cheap resources will earn profits; firms conserving on expensive resources will avoid losses.

Assuming the conditions in Section 4.5 are met, prices always provide accurate information and appropriate incentives. Since traditional and command economies downplay the role of prices, they have a much more difficult time achieving allocational and technical efficiency.

4.4 ADAM SMITH AND *THE WEALTH OF NATIONS*

Adam Smith—Adam Smith (1723–1790) was a Scottish economist whose writing can be said to have inaugurated the modern era of economic analysis.

The Wealth of Nations—Published in 1776, *The Wealth of Nations* can be read as an analysis of a market economy. It was Smith's belief that a market economy was a superior form of organization from the standpoint of both economic progress and human liberty.

Invisible Hand—Smith acknowledged that self-interest was a dominant motivating force in a market economy, yet this self-interest was ultimately consistent with the public interest. Market participants were guided by an invisible hand to act in ways that promoted the public interest. Firms may only be concerned with profits, but profits are only earned by firms that satisfy consumer demand and keep costs down.

4.5 CONDITIONS THAT MUST BE MET FOR A MARKET ECONOMY TO ACHIEVE ALLOCATIVE AND TECHNICAL EFFICIENCY

A market economy will automatically produce the optimum quantity of every good or service at the lowest possible cost if four conditions are met:

Adequate Information—Consumers must be well-enough informed about prices, quality and availability of products, and other matters that they can make intelligent spending decisions. Workers must be well-enough informed about wages and working conditions that they can choose wisely among job opportunities. Other segments of the economy must be similarly well-informed.

Competition—There must be vigorous competition in every market. Monopolistic elements will reduce output, raise prices, and allow inefficiency in particular markets.

No Externalities—Externalities exist when a transaction between a buyer and seller affects an innocent third party. An example would be if *A* buys a product from *B* that *B* produced under conditions that polluted the air that others breathe. (Not all externalities result in damage to society. Some are beneficial.) Where externalities are present, there is the possibility of over- or under-production of particular good and services.

No Public Goods—The market is unlikely to produce the appropriate quantity of public goods for reasons discussed in Chapter 5.

4.6 APTNESS OF THE MARKET ECONOMY MODEL

Critics from all points on the political spectrum have criticized the market economy model as a description of both the structure and performance of the American economy.

From the standpoint of structure, some of the major problems they point out include:

1. The existence of gigantic firms and limitations on competi-

tion in many important markets.

2. The perceived widespread existence of externalities.

3. The size and intrusiveness of government.

4. Consumer and worker ignorance.

From the standpoint of performance, major problems they point to include:

1. Extended periods of high unemployment, high inflation, and sluggish growth.

2. The perception of dramatic inequality in income and wealth.

3. Anecdotal evidence of corruption, abuse of power, and wasteful practices in business.

Even supporters of the model admit that it is highly simplified. Students must decide for themselves whether the abstract model is insightful or misleading.

CHAPTER 5

THE PRIVATE SECTOR OF
THE AMERICAN ECONOMY

PRIVATE SECTOR

The private sector refers to households and privately-owned businesses.

5.1 HOUSEHOLDS

A household is defined as a group of people living in the same residence. Households are buyers of goods and services, savers and borrowers, and owners and suppliers of resources to firms. There are approximately 80,000,000 households in the United States.

5.2 TYPES OF BUSINESS ORGANIZATION

Firms—Business firms buy or rent resources, save and invest in capital equipment, and produce goods and services. There are approximately 16,000,000 firms in the United States.

Proprietorship—A proprietorship is a business form where one individual owns and manages the firm and is solely and personally responsible for all debts incurred by the firm. Major advantages are that:

1. They are easy to establish.

2. The owner has absolute control over the direction her firm takes.

Disadvantages include:

1. Limitations on size—Proprietorships tend to be small because they must rely on the capital of only one individual and there are limits to how much one person can manage.

2. Unlimited liability—The full debt of the firm becomes the **personal** responsibility of the proprietor.

3. Limited life—The proprietorship dies when the owner dies.

There are approximately 11,000,000 proprietorships in the United States.

Partnership—A partnership is a business form where two or more individuals own and manage a firm. There are several advantages of the partnership form:

1. They are easy to establish.

2. They tend to be larger than proprietorships because they draw on more than one source of capital and can employ cooperative management.

Disadvantages include:

1. Unlimited liability—Each partner is **personally** and **fully** liable for all debts of the business. If your partners skip out to Brazil, you may have to cover all the business debts.

2. Decision-making gets progressively harder as the number of partners increases.

3. Like the proprietorship, a partnership dies when any one of the partners die.

There are approximately 2,000,000 partnerships in the United States.

Corporation—A corporation is a business form with characteristics established by law. Corporations must obtain a corporate charter from a state government. This charter provides the right to do business and gives the corporation many of the legal rights enjoyed by persons. Corporations raise their initial capital (and sometimes later infusions) by selling shares of stock. The stockholders (shareholders) become the owners of the corporation with ownership rights based on the amount of stock owned.

Advantages of the corporate form include:

1. Large size—There is virtually no limit to the amount of capital a corporation can raise.

2. Limited liability—Stockholders are liable for corporate debts only to the extent of their stock investment.

3. Unlimited Life—Corporations can continue even if their initial owners die.

4. Legal Rights—In the United States, corporations enjoy most of the legal rights of persons.

Disadvantages include:

1. Double Taxation—Government taxes corporate profits directly and indirectly by taxing profit shares paid out to owners.

There are 3,000,000 corporations in the United States.

Conglomerate—A conglomerate is a business firm that competes in two or more unrelated industries.

Multinational—A multinational is a firm that has factories or offices in more than one country.

INDUSTRY

An industry is a group of firms that produce the same or a similar product. Some industries consist of only one firm.

Industrial Policy—Industrial policy refers to a wide variety of government policies that can be used to enhance or protect the productivity and competitive position of domestic industries and firms. Often a specific goal is to improve the ability of domestic industries or firms to withstand foreign competition or compete in foreign markets. Another common goal is to create more high-paying jobs and increase the rate of growth of the economy. Examples of these policies include protection against imports, government financial support for research and development, exemptions from antitrust restrictions, and government allocation of financial capital.

ANTITRUST

Antitrust refers to a series of laws that attempt to promote greater competition in the private business sector.

5.3   DISTRIBUTION OF INCOME AND WEALTH

Wealth—Wealth is anything you own of value. What makes wealth valuable is that it provides to its owner goods, services, or money. Examples of wealth would be stocks and bonds, real estate, a bank account, education and work skills, farm animals, and great paintings. The amount of wealth a person possesses is measured at a particular point in time. This makes wealth a stock variable.

STOCK VARIABLE

An economic variable that can only be meaningfully measured at a particular point in time.

Net Worth—An individual's net worth is the difference between the value of his wealth and his debts. It too is a stock variable.

Income—Income is the goods, services, or money that wealth provides. Examples of income are dividends and interest payments from stocks and bonds, the pleasures of living in your own house, interest payments and convenience from a bank account, wages and salaries from education and work skills, milk and meat from farm animals, and the enjoyment of viewing a great painting. The amount of income a person receives is measured over a particular period of time, for example a week, month, or year. This makes income a flow variable. Some forms of income cannot be easily measured, such as the enjoyment from great paintings, and are typically excluded from analyses of people's incomes.

Compensation of Employees	$2,904.7
Proprietor's Income	324.5
Rent	19.3
Corporate Profits	328.1
Interest	391.5
National Income	$3,968.2

Source: *Survey of Current Business*
all figures in billions

TABLE 5.1–Functional Distribution of Income, 1988

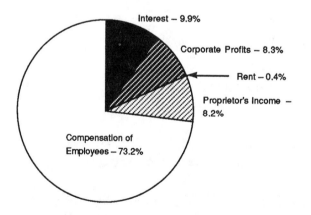

FIGURE 5.1–Functional Distribution of Income

39

Functional Distribution of Income—The functional distribution of income shows national income broken down by the type of resource that earned it (see Table 5.1 and Figure 5.1). Wages, rent, interest, proprietor's income and corporate profits can, somewhat loosely, be thought of as the returns to labor, land, capital, and entrepreneurship.

Personal Distribution of Income—The personal distribution of income shows the distribution among households (see Table 5.2). An obvious conclusion is that income is distributed far from equally in the United States.

Income Range	Percent of Households
<$2,500	2.3
$2,500–4,999	4.6
$5,000–7,499	6.3
$7,500–9,999	5.2
$10,000–12,499	5.6
$12,500–14,999	5.0
$15,000–19,999	10.0
$20,000–24,999	9.2
$25,000–34,999	16.1
$35,000–49,999	17.2
>$50,000	18.5
Median Household Income	$25,986
Mean Household Income	$32,144

TABLE 5.2–Personal Distribution of Income by Households, 1988

Trends in Median Family Income—In 1987 median family income was $30,853, the highest level on record. The graph shows family income adjusted for changes in the purchasing power of the dollar. After increasing on average 4.0% a year from 1947 to 1973, family income fell below the 1973 level of $30,820, not passing that level until 1987.

MEDIAN FAMILY INCOME

The median income is the one right in the middle. Half the families make more and half make less.

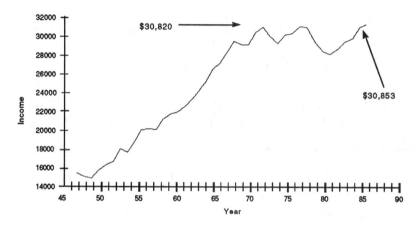

FIGURE 5.2–Trends in Median Family Income

POVERTY RATE

The poverty rate measures the proportion of the population that is considered poor. A person is considered poor if she lives in a household that receives less than a certain amount of money income for a household of that size. The poverty line for a household of four in 1987 was $11,611.

Trends in the Poverty Rate—After falling fairly steadily from 1959 through 1973, the poverty rate turned back up. Only recently has the rate resumed a downward movement.

41

Figure 5.3

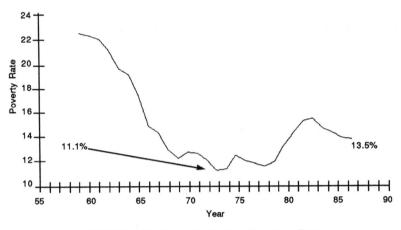

FIGURE 5.3–Trends in the Poverty Rate

The Distribution of Wealth—Wealth as measured by net worth is distributed unequally in the United States as Table 5.3 shows.

Net Worth	Percent of Families	
<$5,000	33.0	
$5,000–9,999	5.0	
$10,000–24,999	12.0	
$25,000–49,999	16.0	
$50,000–99,999	17.0	
$100,000–249,999	12.0	
$250,000–499,999	3.0	
>$500,000	2.0	
Median Net Worth		$24,575
Mean Net Worth		$66,050

Source: *Federal Reserve Bulletin*

TABLE 5.3–Distribution of Family Net Worth, 1983

CHAPTER 6

THE PUBLIC SECTOR IN THE AMERICAN ECONOMY

PUBLIC SECTOR

The Public Sector refers to the activities of government.

6.1 GOVERNMENT SPENDING

Government Expenditures on Goods and Services v. Transfer Payments—Government spending can be usefully broken down into two categories. One category is spending on goods and services. When government buys a battleship, typewriter, or the Space Shuttle, it is acquiring goods. When government pays the salary of a soldier, teacher or bureaucrat, it is getting a service in return. The second category is transfer payments. Transfers are money or in-kind items given to individuals or businesses for which the government receives no equivalent good or service in return. Examples would be social security payments, welfare, or unemployment compensation.

Functional Breakdown of Spending Side of Federal Budget—

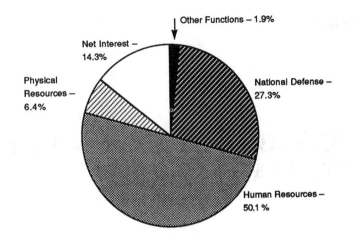

FIGURE 6.1–Federal Expenditures by Category, 1988

Functional Breakdown of Spending Side of State and Local Government Budgets—

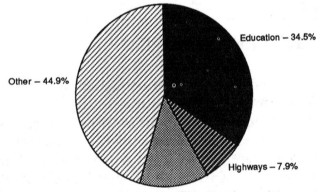

FIGURE 6.2–State and Local Government Spending by Category, 1988

6.2 TAXES

Average Tax Rate–The average tax rate (ATR) is the proportion of income paid in taxes.

$$ ATR = \frac{Taxes}{Income} $$

Marginal Tax Rate—The marginal tax rate (MTR) is the proportion of each additional dollar paid in taxes.

$$ MTR = \frac{\Delta Taxes}{\Delta Income} $$

Progressive Tax System—A progressive tax system is one where taxpayers with higher incomes pay a higher average tax rate. In the table, as income rises, not only are more taxes paid, but taxes are paid at a higher rate. An important feature of such a tax system is that the marginal tax rate increases as the level of income rises.

Taxable Income	20,000	22,000	24,000	26,000	28,000	30,000	32,000
Tax	2,000	2,300	2,700	3,200	3,800	4,500	5,300
ATR	.100	.105	.113	.123	.136	.150	.166
MTR	—	.150	.200	.250	.300	.350	.400

Proportional Tax System—A proportional tax system is one where all taxpayers pay the same average tax rate. In the table, as income rises, taxes paid increase, but taxes are paid at the same rate. An important feature of such a tax system is that the marginal tax rate is always equal to the average tax rate, and, consequently, remains the same as the level of income rises.

Taxable Income	20,000	22,000	24,000	26,000	28,000	30,000	32,000
Tax	3,000	3,300	3,600	3,900	4,200	4,500	4,800
ATR	.150	.150	.150	.150	.150	.150	.150
MTR	—	.150	.150	.150	.150	.150	.150

Regressive Tax System—A regressive tax system is one where taxpayers with higher incomes pay a lower average tax rate. In the table, as income rises, taxes paid rise but the average tax rate falls. An important feature of such a tax system is that the marginal tax rate decreases as the level of income rises.

Taxable Income	20,000	22,000	24,000	26,000	28,000	30,000	32,000
Tax	2,000	2,190	2,370	2,540	2,700	2,850	2,990
ATR	.100	.099	.098	.097	.096	.095	.093
MTR	—	.095	.090	.085	.080	.075	.070

User Charges—User charges are fees that individuals pay for the use of government services or to buy goods produced by government. Examples are entrance fees to national parks and charges for government documents purchased from the Government Printing Office.

6.3   CHARACTERISTICS OF A GOOD TAX

In addition to raising revenue, a good tax has the following characteristics:

Horizontal Equity—Horizontal equity is achieved when equals are treated equally, i.e., when individuals with similar circumstances are taxed the same.

Vertical Equity—Vertical equity is achieved when unequals are treated unequally, i.e., when individuals with different circumstances pay different amounts of tax.

46

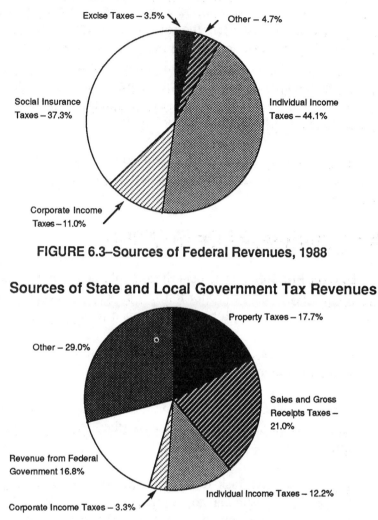

Sources of Federal Tax Revenues

Excise Taxes – 3.5%

Other – 4.7%

Social Insurance Taxes – 37.3%

Individual Income Taxes – 44.1%

Corporate Income Taxes – 11.0%

FIGURE 6.3–Sources of Federal Revenues, 1988

Sources of State and Local Government Tax Revenues

Property Taxes – 17.7%

Other – 29.0%

Sales and Gross Receipts Taxes – 21.0%

Revenue from Federal Government 16.8%

Corporate Income Taxes – 3.3%

Individual Income Taxes – 12.2%

FIGURE 6.4–Sources of State and Local Revenues, 1988

Incentives—If the allocation of resources yielded by a pure market system is considered ideal, then a good tax is one that would not change the actual allocation away from what the market would cause, or which would return the actual allocation to what the market would cause.

47

In the context of current American policy discussions, a good tax is one that does not adversely affect the decisions to work, save, and invest. Here the role of the marginal tax rate is considered crucial. The higher the marginal tax rate, the less an individual can keep out of any additional income earned. Consequently, a fear is that systems with marginal tax rates that are "too high" will lead to less work, saving, and investment, and a lower standard of living for that society.

Simplicity—Everything else held equal, systems that are easier to understand and require less effort to comply with are preferred.

6.4 PRINCIPLES OF TAXATION

Benefit Principle—The benefit principle says that individuals should pay taxes in proportion to the benefits they receive from government. The problems with this principle include:

1. Not all taxpayers can afford the benefits they receive, e.g., welfare recipients.

2. Taxpayers have an incentive to understate the benefits they receive from government programs (the "free-rider" problem).

3. It is not an easy task to measure the benefits individuals receive from particular government programs, e.g., putting a monetary value on the benefits received from national defense.

Ability-to-Pay Principle—The ability-to-pay principle says that individuals should pay taxes based on their income or wealth (i.e., "ability-to-pay"). The rationale is that the most well-off have the most to lose if government does not function correctly. The problems with this principle include:

1. The equity issue of making people pay for services they do not receive.

2. The incentive problem associated with essentially penalizing people for being successful.

3. Determining the exact amount each person should pay.

6.5 DEFICITS, SURPLUSES, AND THE PUBLIC DEBT

Budget Deficits—The government's budget is in deficit when its spending exceeds the amount of revenue brought in from taxes and user charges. To finance the spending in excess of revenues, the government borrows. The amount borrowed is equal to the deficit.

Budget Surpluses—The government's budget is in surplus when its spending is less than the amount of revenue brought in from taxes and user charges. The excess revenue can be used to pay back previous borrowing.

Public (National) Debt—The money government borrows to finance a deficit establishes the public's debt. Since the government has run more deficits than surpluses, the public debt has grown over time. Typically, government borrows money for long periods of time. Ten, twenty, and thirty year loans are not uncommon. These loans remain part of the public debt until they are paid. Even then, most loans that come due are paid back by borrowing from another source (refinancing) so, in a sense, the public debt is never paid back.

6.6 ROLE OF GOVERNMENT

Public Goods and Services—Public goods and services have the following characteristics:

1. **Nonrival**—Consumption of the item by one person does not reduce the amount available for others to consume, or, equivalently, everyone can consume all of the item.

2. **Nonexclusion**—Nonpayers cannot be prevented from consuming the item.

The classic example of a public good is national defense. It is a nonrival good because the amount I consume of defense does not reduce the amount available for you to consume. We both consume our entire system of national defense. Also, national defense is nonexclusive. Assuming a system is in place, everyone in the country is protected, regardless of whether they have paid for it or not.

The opposite of a public good or service is a **private good or service**. The latter is both a rival and an exclusive good. It is rival because consumption by one reduces the amount available for all others, and it is exclusive because nonpayers can be prevented from consuming. A good example would be a soft drink. If I drink a can of soda, you cannot drink the same can. If you do not buy a can, you cannot enjoy the product.

Although a complete explanation would have to await microeconomics, economists believe that public goods will probably not be adequately supplied by the market. One of the main reasons stems from nonexclusion. Since you consume the good whether you pay or not, what is the incentive to pay? Consumers will rationally attempt to become "free riders," and the market would be unable to support a public good. Consequently, government is required to provide the good because government can do one thing the market cannot, it can compel people to pay. Also, and this point will be made without explanation, the nonrival characteristic implies that public goods and services should carry a price of $0, something that the market could obviously not support.

The existence of public goods and services provides a rationale for some government participation in the economy. The fact that government may be required to supply some goods and services does not imply government will always do a flawless job of it.

Merit Goods and Services—Merit goods and services are items that the government supplies because it thinks they are in the best interest of the public, whether the public demands the goods or not. An example is public television. It is highly unlikely that most of these shows could survive in the marketplace because there is not adequate viewer support.

Externalities—Externalities occur when a market transaction between two parties affects a third party who was not included in the transaction. An example would be if I buy a product from a producer whose production process pollutes the air that everyone breathes. The problem is that the effect on third parties is frequently ignored, to the detriment of third parties. Government action is frequently called for to rectify the damages to third parties or prevent the externality from happening. An example would be government regulation of pollution.

Conservative view of the proper role of government—In the American context, a conservative in economic matters tends to believe the following:

a. The **performance**, if not structure, of our economy closely resembles that of a pure market economy.

b. The distribution of income and wealth is proportional to individual contributions to the economy, and hence, is quite equitable.

c. As a consequence, the need for government participation in the economy is quite limited.

d. Government is inherently inefficient and its actions are frequently inequitable.

e. Most of our major economic problems can be traced to misguided government policies. For example, inflation and recession is largely caused by mismanaged fiscal and monetary policy, unemployment largely reflects government policies that reduce wage flexibility, sluggish growth is the result of too high tax rates and overregulation.

Liberal view of the proper role of government—In the American context, a liberal in economic matters tends to believe the following:

a. Both in structure and performance, our economy does not resemble a pure market economy. Widespread monopoly and externalities and consumer and worker ignorance leads to inefficiency.

b. The distribution of income and wealth is distorted by economic power and widespread discrimination, and hence, cannot be considered equitable. In addition, strict adherence to a contributory standard in an economy characterized by a high degree of specialization and interdependence cannot be justified.

c. As a consequence, widespread government participation in the economy is required to fight monopoly and discrimination, protect consumers and workers, and redistribute income.

d. With the exercise of proper care, government is capable of successfully carrying out its duties.

e. Greater government intervention in the economy has led to better performance. Major economic problems are the result of too little government oversight, not too much.

Public Choice—Public Choice is one of the newest fields within the discipline of economics. It applies economic methodology to analyze the actions of governments, politicians, and bureaucrats.

CHAPTER 7

GROSS NATIONAL PRODUCT

7.1 MEASURING GNP

Gross National Product—Gross National Product (or GNP) is a measure of the dollar value of final goods and services produced by the economy over a given period of time, usually one year. It is the most comprehensive indicator of the economy's health available, although it is not a measure of society's overall well-being.

Final Goods and Services—Final goods and services are those sold to their ultimate users.

Intermediate Goods and Services—Intermediate goods and services are those in an intermediate stage of processing. They are purchased by firms for immediate resale, such as the frozen orange juice a grocery store buys from the processor for resale to consumers or they are purchased for further processing and then resale, such as the crude oil a refinery buys to refine into gasoline and other petroleum products.

GNP in the Circular Flow—Assume a simple economy composed of three business firms and one household. Firm A manufactures computer chips. It takes silicon from the environment (assumed to be so plentiful as to be a free good), and combines it with resources purchased or rented from the household. The resulting chips are sold to Firm B, a manufacturer of computers. Firm B takes the chips and combines them with the resources purchased from the household to produce computers which it sells to firm C, a retail computer store. The store uses resources obtained from the household to resell the computers to the household, which is the ultimate user.

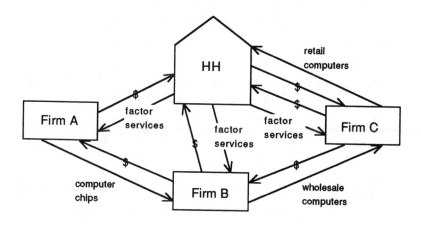

FIGURE 7.1–GNP in the Circular Flow

The table traces the transactions that take place in the economy during the course of a year.

Firm	Cost of Intermediate Goods Purchased	Resources Purchased	Cost of Goods Sold	Value-Added
A	0	50	50	50
B	50	75	125	75
C	125	40	165	40

55

There are three ways to measure GNP.

1. **Expenditures on Final Goods and Services**—In the example, computer chips and wholesale computers are intermediate goods while retail computers are a final good. Since the household spent $165 on retail computers, this is a direct measure of GNP.

2. **Sum of Value-Added for All Firms**—

Value-Added (VA) = Cost of Goods Sold – Cost of Intermediate Goods Purchased

---

VA measures the value of the processing and resale activities that the firm performs on the intermediate goods and services it purchases. Adding value-added for all firms in the economy will give GNP. It follows because the value of final goods and services produced results from the contributions of all firms at all stages of the production process.

3. **Gross National Income**—Where does value-added come from? It comes from the services performed by the resources the firms hires. Therefore, value-added for each firm is just equal to the payments made for resources allowing us to total the incomes earned by all households to get GNP. This measure is frequently given the name Gross National Income (or GNI).

Trends in GNP—GNP rose from $91.3 billion in 1939 to $4,864.3 billion in 1988, although the rise was far from smooth and steady (see Figure 7.2).

7.2 NOMINAL vs. REAL VALUES

A nation's GNP is measured in terms of its national cur-

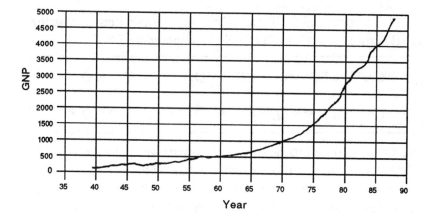

FIGURE 7.2–Trends in GNP

rency. In the United States, GNP is measured in dollars. The reason is to have a common unit to measure disparate goods. It is impossible to add 10 bushes of apples and 30 crates of oranges, but we can add $60 of applies and $100 of oranges. What this means is we must compute the market value of each good or service produced.

Market Value = Market Price of Good or Service × Quantity

Nominal GNP—Nominal GNP (or current dollar GNP or money GNP) is GNP computed by using the current year's market price for each product. For example, nominal GNP in 1989 is computed using the quantity produced of each good or service and the price each good or service sold for during the year.

$$GNP^{89} = P_1{}^{89} \times Q_1{}^{89} + P_2{}^{89} \times Q_2{}^{89} + \ldots + P_n{}^{89} \times Q_n{}^{89}$$

where the subscripts refer to all the different goods and services produced, and the superscripts refer to the year.

Use of nominal GNP can create problems when comparing GNP across time. Consider GNP^{89} compared to GNP^{80}.

$$GNP^{80} = P_1^{80} \times Q_1^{80} + P_2^{80} \times Q_2^{80} + \ldots + P_n^{80} \times Q_n^{80}$$

$$GNP^{89} = P_1^{89} \times Q_1^{89} + P_2^{89} \times Q_2^{89} + \ldots + P_n^{89} \times Q_n^{89}$$

Presumably, the purpose of GNP comparisons is to see whether GNP has grown, or, more exactly, whether the economy's output of goods and services has increased (the Q's). Yet GNP could have grown between 1980 and 1989 just due to increases in prices (the P's).

Real GNP—Real GNP (or constant dollar GNP) is GNP computed using the market prices from a selected base year. For example, assume 1980 is selected as the base year. Then GNP is computed for every year using the 1980 prices.

$$GNP^{80} = P_1^{80} \times Q_1^{80} + P_2^{80} \times Q_2^{80} + \ldots + P_n^{80} \times Q_n^{80}$$

$$GNP^{89} = P_1^{80} \times Q_1^{89} + P_2^{80} \times Q_2^{89} + \ldots + P_n^{80} \times Q_n^{89}$$

Real GNP facilitates comparisons of GNP across years. If a common set of prices is used, GNP will only appear to have grown if the actual output of goods and services has increased (the Q's).

EXAMPLE

	Bread			Soda Pop			
	P	Q	PQ	P	Q	PQ	GNP
Nominal[80]	2.00	150	300	1.00	500	500	800
Nominal[89]	2.20	200	440	1.10	600	660	1100
Real[89]	2.00	200	400	1.00	600	600	1000

> **BASE YEAR**
>
> A base year is an arbitrarily chosen year which is used as the basis of comparison in an analysis.

GNP Deflator—The GNP deflator is a measure of the average price level in a given year. The GNP deflator for the base year is always given the value 100. The deflator for earlier and later years is proportionately scaled up or down based on the percentage change in the average price level. For example, if the deflator was 108 in the year after the base year, the average level of prices would have risen by 8%.

> GNP Deflator^{xx} = (Nominal GNP^{xx}/Real GNP^{xx}) $\times$ 100

Using the data from the table:

$$\text{GNP Deflator}^{89} = (1100/1000) \times 100 = 110$$

The GNP deflator can be used to "deflate" nominal GNP data into real terms.

> Real GNP^{xx} = (Nominal GNP^{xx}/GNP Deflator^{xx}) $\times$ 100

Using the data from the table:

$$\text{Real GNP}^{89} = (1100/110) \times 100 = 1000$$

7.3 PROBLEMS WITH MEASURING GNP

Market v. Non-market Production—Since GNP measures the market value of final goods and services, only those goods and services that have been sold in markets can be included in

GNP. This excludes a not insignificant amount of our nation's production. Examples of excluded production would be the produce of backyard vegetable gardens, the home services performed by homemakers, all do-it-yourself activities, and criminal activity.

Second-Hand Goods—GNP is a measure of our current production of goods and services. This means sales of already produced items, such as used cars, are not included.

Assets—GNP does not measure the value of our national and personal assets.

GNP as a Measure of Social Welfare—GNP is only a measure of production. While goods and services certainly contribute to human happiness, they are not all that is needed. GNP does not measure the value of the love, caring and friendship in society, or take account of available leisure. Also, it includes some production that arguably does not lead to greater happiness. For example, if there is a crime wave and society produces more burglar alarms, GNP will go up although society is probably not better off.

7.4   COMPONENTS OF GNP AND GNI

Components of GNP and GNI, 1988

GNP

Personal Consumption Expenditures	$3,227.5
Gross Private Domestic Investment	766.5
Government Purchases of Goods and Services	964.9
Net Exports	−94.6
	$4,864.3

GNI

Compensation of Employees	$2,904.7
Proprietor's Income	324.5
Rent	19.3
Corporate Profits	328.1
Interest	391.5
Capital Consumption Allowance	506.3
Indirect Business Taxes	389.9
	$4,864.3

Personal Consumption Expenditures (C)—This category includes all spending by households, with the exception of purchases of new homes. An interesting inclusion is the imputed value of owner-occupied housing, one of the few examples of non-market production in GNP.

Gross Private Domestic Investment (I)—This category includes private business spending for new capital equipment, **changes** in business inventories, and household purchases of new homes.

Why Gross Investment?—Investment spending can take place to replace capital goods that have worn out (called replacement investment) or to add to the stock of capital goods (called net investment). Gross investment is the sum of replacement and net.

Why "Changes in Inventory"?—Inventory refers to already produced goods that are being stored in anticipation of later sale. Changes in inventory are included in GNP to allow us to distinguish production from sales and get an accurate measure of GNP.

Assume on January 1 businesses hold inventories of $80 billion, consisting of goods that were produced in the past but unsold. Assume further that during the year $5,000 billion of final goods and services were produced, but only $4,900 billion of these were sold. The unsold $100 billion goes into inventory so on December 31, inventories stand at $180 billion. The correct measure of GNP is $5,000 billion, but if we only measure sales we will fall short. Consequently we must add the **change** in inventories ($180 billion − $80 billion = $100 billion) to the sales to get an accurate count of GNP.

Inv = $80 bill	produce $5,000 bill	Inv = $180 bill
Jan. 1	sell $4,900 billion	Dec. 31

Government Spending on Goods and Services (G)— All government (federal, state, and local) purchases of goods and services are included in this category. This does not include transfer payments, since transfers do not signify current production.

Net Exports of Goods and Services (X − M)—Net Exports = Exports (X) − Imports (M). Even though our nation does not get to consume the goods and services we sell to foreign countries, exports are included because they are part of our production. Imports are included under consumption but must be subtracted here because they do not represent our production. International flows of assets are not included here.

Compensation of Employees—This category includes all wages, salaries, and supplements. Supplements are aspects of employee compensation that do not show up in the paycheck, such as employer contributions to social security.

Rent—This category includes landlord incomes and sundry other items.

Interest—This category measures the income earned from lending money.

Proprietor's Income—The income earned by businesses that are not corporations is proprietor's income.

Corporate Profits—The profits of corporations.

Indirect Business Taxes—These are taxes paid by business that are not levied on sales or income. Examples would be property taxes and license fees.

Capital Consumption Allowances—This is an estimate of the value of capital depreciation in the economy.

DEPRECIATION

Capital goods "wear down" with use or time. Depreciation is an estimate of this reduction in value and is a cost of production.

7.5 OTHER MEASURES OF INCOME

Net National Product—

Gross National Product	$4,864.3
− Capital Consumption Allowances	−506.3
Net National Product	$4,358.0

NNP measures current production of goods and services less any replacement investment. Since replacement investment does not measure "forward progress" for the economy, NNP may be conceptually a superior measure of the state of the economy than GNP. Since Capital Consumption Allowance data is such a crude estimate of actual depreciation, NNP is not widely used.

National Income—

Net National Product	$4,358.0
− Indirect Business Taxes	−389.9
National Income	$3,968.2

(figures may not add-up due to rounding)

NI measures the income earned by factors of production.

Personal Income—

National Income	$3,968.2
− Income earned but not received	−1,164.3
+ Income received but not earned	+1,258.2
Personal Income	$4,062.1

Examples of income earned but not received would be employer supplements to wages and salaries and some payroll taxes. Income taxes are not subtracted here (although they fit the definition). An example of income received but not earned would be transfer payments to households. An advantage of personal income is that data is available monthly.

Disposable Income—

Personal Income	$4,062.1
− Personal Taxes	−590.3
Disposable Income	$3,471.8

DI is the income households have available to spend or save as they please.

CHAPTER 8

MACROECONOMIC PROBLEMS OF THE AMERICAN ECONOMY

8.1   THE BUSINESS CYCLE

Business Cycles—Business cycles are the alternating periods of prosperity and recession that seem to characterize all market-oriented economies.

Four Phases of the Cycle—Every business cycle consists of four phases. The peak is the high point of business activity. It occurs at a specific point of time. The contraction is a period of declining business activity. It occurs over a period of time. The trough is the low point in business activity. It, too, occurs at a specific point in time. The expansion is a period of growing business activity. It takes place over a period of time.

Although the word cycle implies a certain uniformity, that is misleading. Each business cycle differs from every other in terms of duration of contractions and expansions, and height of peak and depth of trough.

Seasonal Fluctuations—Seasonal fluctuations are changes

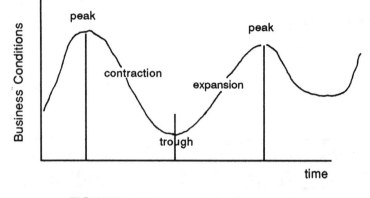

FIGURE 8.1–Phases of the Business Cycle

in economic variables that reflect the season of the year. For example, every summer ice cream sales soar. They decrease during winter. Every December, toy sales increase dramatically. They fall back during January.

Secular Trends —A secular trend is the long run direction of movement of a variable. For example, our economy has become dramatically richer over the past century. We can say that there was a secular upward trend in real GNP. Of course,

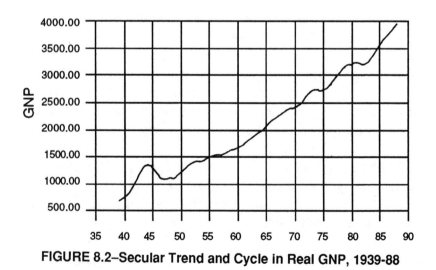

FIGURE 8.2–Secular Trend and Cycle in Real GNP, 1939-88

66

growth was not steady. There were periods of faster than average followed by slower than average growth, which accounts for business cycles.

8.2 UNEMPLOYMENT

Employment—A person is employed when they have a job. In the United States, only one hour of paid work a week is sufficient to be considered employed.

Unemployment—People are considered unemployed when they are without a job and **actively seeking** one. Active seeking includes such behaviors as reading want ads, contacting employers, and using the services of the Public Employment Agencies.

Labor Force—The labor force consists of all people who have a job or would like a job and are actively seeking one. In short, the labor force consists of all employed and unemployed people.

Labor Force Participation Rate—The labor force participation rate (LFPR) is the percentage of the population in the labor force.

$$\text{LFPR} = \frac{\text{Labor Force}}{\text{Population}}$$

Unemployment Rate—The unemployment rate is the number of unemployed people as a percentage of the **labor force**.

$$\text{Unemployment Rate} = \frac{\text{Unemployed}}{\text{Labor Force}}$$

Employment Rate—The employment rate is the number of employed people as a percentage of the **population**.

$$\text{Employment Rate} = \frac{\text{Employed}}{\text{Population}}$$

Full Employment—Full employment is not a situation where the employment is 100%, or the unemployment rate is 0%. There is some unemployment at full employment. While no one can say for sure what the full employment unemployment rate is, most economists believe full employment is obtained when the unemployment rate is in the 4-5.5% range. At full employment, the number of vacant jobs is just equal to the number of unemployed people. The unemployed just have not located the jobs or lack the required skills. Since there is neither a shortage or surplus of labor, wages should remain stationary at full employment.

Natural Rate of Unemployment—The natural rate of unemployment can be defined in three equivalent ways:

1. It is the level of unemployment at which the expected rate of inflation equals the actual rate.

2. It is the level of unemployment at which the labor market is in equilibrium.

3. It is "true" full employment.

Frictional Unemployment—The frictionally unemployed are workers who are "between jobs." These are workers who have quit, been fired, or been laid off due to a decline in a firm or industry, or just entered the labor force. They likely will find a new job in a reasonable amount of time, but they have not found one yet. Some frictional unemployment is to be expected since labor market information (location of job vacancies, characteristics of job, etc.) tends to be limited. Frictional unemployment is found at full employment, but its level is influenced by the availability of job market information.

Structural Unemployment—The structurally unemployed are workers who lack the skills to fill available job vacancies. Some structural unemployment is inevitable in a dynamic economy. Structural unemployment is found at full employment, but its level could be influenced by the availability of retraining opportunities.

Cyclical Unemployment—The cyclically unemployed are workers who have lost their jobs due to a downturn in the business cycle.

Discouraged Workers—Discouraged workers are people who are without a job, want a job, but have looked unsuccessfully for such a long time that they have, in effect, "given up" the search. Officially, they are counted as "not in the labor force" because they are not actively seeking work, but they do want a job. During deep recessions and in some areas of the countries at all times, the number of discouraged workers can be considerable.

8.3 INFLATION

Inflation—Inflation is a sustained, substantial increase in the average level of prices.

Deflation—Deflation is a sustained, substantial decrease in the average level of prices.

Disinflation—Disinflation refers to a decrease in the rate of inflation.

Stagflation—Stagflation refers to a period of time when both the unemployment and inflation rates are high.

Hyperinflation—Hyperinflation refers to a period of extremely rapid inflation.

Consumer Price Index—Sometimes called the Cost of Living Index, the Consumer Price Index (or CPI) attempts to measure the cost of living for a typical family.

The initial step in constructing the CPI is to define a "market basket" of goods and services. The market basket is a representative sample of the goods and services that a typical family would buy over a given period of time. The cost of the market basket can be computed at different points in time. Changes in the cost of the market basket are taken to measure changes in the cost of living. Typically, the cost of the market basket is expressed in price index terms. The cost is given the arbitrary value of 100 in the arbitrarily chosen base year. The index is then scaled up or down proportionally in earlier or later periods of time.

	Year 1		Year 2	
	P	Cost	P	Cost
50 loaves bread	2.00	100.00	2.10	105.00
100 bottles soda	1.00	100.00	1.10	110.00
		200.00		215.00

Constructing the Consumer Price Index

In the table above, the market basket consists of 50 loaves of bread and 100 bottles of soda pop. In year 1, they cost $2.00 per loaf and $1.00 per bottle, respectively, for a total cost of $200. In year 2, the prices of both products and, consequently, the market basket rise. The new market basket cost of $215 is

7.5% greater than in year 1 (($215 – $200)/$200 = 0.75). Therefore we conclude that the cost of living rose 7.5% between year 1 and year 2.

In index number terms, if we let the $200 cost in year 1 be represented by 100, then the $215 will be represented by 107.5. The price index for year 2 can be found by solving a ratio problem.

Year2/Year1 = $215/$200 = X/100,

where X is the unknown index number for Year 2 and 100 is the base year index.

Index Number Mathematics

One use of the CPI is to "deflate" nominal consumer incomes into their equivalent in purchasing power:

Purchasing Power of Income = (Nominal Income/CPI) × 100

For example, assume a consumer's nominal income was $30,000 in Year 1, our base year. Because it is the base year, the $30,000 is taken to have a purchasing power of $30,000 (($30,000/100) × 100). Assume the consumer's income rises to $34,000 in Year 2. Does this necessarily mean the consumer's purchasing power has risen by $4,000 or 13.34%? Can the consumer buy 13.34% more goods and services than she did in Year 1? If the prices rose between the two years, then the answer must be no. The nominal increase in Year 2 has a purchasing power of $31,627.91 (($34,000/107.5) × 100), which is only 5.43% greater than in Year 1. The interpretation of this result is that because of higher prices, $34,000 in Year 2 could only buy as much as $31,627.91 in Year 1.

Problems with the CPI—The CPI should be recognized as only a rough measure of the cost of living.

1. The index is constructed for the "typical family." Since no family is typical, the index will be inaccurate. For example, if your family normally consumes 45 loaves of bread and 110 bottles of soda pop, your cost of living would increase more than the index indicates because you are consuming relatively more of the item whose cost has increased relatively more.

	Year 1		Year 2	
	P	Cost	P	Cost
45 loaves bread	$2.00	$ 90.00	$2.10	$ 94.50
110 bottles soda	$1.00	$110.00	$1.10	$121.00
		$200.00		$215.50

CPI = $215.50/$200.00 = X/100, where X = 107.75 in Year 2

Construction of CPI for an atypical family

2. The index does not take into account the fact that people will alter their market basket in response to changes in prices. For example, if soda increased more than bread, people may respond by purchasing less of the relatively more expensive soda and more of the relatively cheaper bread.

3. The market basket is not adjusted for changes in the quality of products. Some price increases may simply reflect that the product is of higher quality.

4. The market basket is not continually altered to take into account the introduction of new products.

Redistribution of Income and Wealth—A serious problem caused by inflation is capricious redistribution of income and wealth. What is often not appreciated is the following. For every buyer, there is a seller, and every buyer is also a seller. If inflation causes buyers to pay 10% more for products, the same inflation will cause sellers to receive 10% more income. Consequently, society's income in the aggregate must keep pace with price changes. Unfortunately, there are some individuals whose income will lag behind price changes. As a result, they will be made worse off. Of course, there must be some whose income rises faster than inflation and are made better off. (Of course, they will think their increase in well-being is simply a reflection of their hard work and virtue.)

It is understandable that during periods of inflation, people desire to protect the purchasing power of their income. A common tactic of unionized workers is to demand **cost-of-living escalators** in wage contracts. A cost-of-living escalator is a clause requiring that wages be raised automatically as the cost-of-living rises. These escalators are sometimes called **COLA's** for **cost-of-living adjustments**. Another term is that wages are **indexed** to the cost-of-living. Currently Federal Social Security recipients have their benefits indexed to the cost-of-living.

With respect to wealth, individuals who store their wealth in forms whose value does not keep pace with inflation will end up worse off. Money holders are particularly susceptible to inflation problems.

The following example illustrates the problem faced by lenders of money during inflationary times. Assume A (the lender or "creditor") loans $100.00 to B (the borrower or "debtor") for one year at 5% interest. A then is willing to sacrifice $100 in purchasing power for a year in the expectation of having $105.00

(the repaid principal of $100 plus the 5% interest) in purchasing power available in a year. Now assume there is 10% inflation during the year (the price index rises from 100 on January 1 to 110 on December 31). The $105.00 repaid will only have a purchasing power of $95.45 (($105.00/110) × 100). In effect, A will have lost because she was repaid less purchasing power than she expected to receive, and B gained because her cost of borrowing (in terms of purchasing power) was less than expected. The table below summarizes the discussion:

	No Inflation			Inflation		
	Nominal Amount	Pur-chasing Power	Price Index	Nominal Amount	Pur-chasing Power	Price Index
lent, beginning of year	$100.00	$100.00	100	$100.00	$100.00	100
repaid, end of year	$105.00	$105.00	100	$105.00	$ 95.45	110

Is there any way for the creditor to protect herself? What if the creditor could anticipate the inflation and added the 10% rate to the rate of interest charged? As the table shows, charging 15% interest would allow her to receive back approximately the amount of purchasing power she had initially expected. Assuming the debtor also anticipated 10% inflation, she would not resist paying a 15% interest rate because the terms of the loan would be no different than what she would have agreed to with no inflation. Thus, to protect their wealth, creditors will add the expected rate of inflation to the rate of interest they charge. This helps explain why interest rates tend to rise during periods of inflation. Of course, forecasting the rate of inflation is extremely difficult to do, so inflation has a tendency to increase uncertainty which may limit lending and borrowing.

Lender charges 15% interest

	Nominal Amount	Purchasing Power	Price Index
lent, beginning of year	$100.00	$100.00	100
repaid, end of year	$115.00	$104.55	110

Inefficiencies—Inflation can also lead to inefficiency which can reduce national output and the rate of real growth. One source of problems is that an inflationary environment is typically one of great uncertainty. Prices and costs in the future cannot be known, and, consequently, long term planning is disrupted. The impact of this is to reduce investment. Another problem is that the pattern of investment is frequently altered away from productive uses to those that are less productive, but may be a good inflation hedge. For example, speculation in gold and great art is common during inflationary times. A third problem is that people pay inordinate attention to their financial affairs, robbing themselves of time that could be used more productively.

CHAPTER 9

MACROECONOMIC MODELS

9.1 WHAT A GOOD MACROECONOMIC MODEL SHOULD BE ABLE TO DO

A macroeconomic model is an abstract replica of the economy as a whole. A good model needs to be able to explain many phenomena, but there are four of particular importance:

1. Business cycles

2. Prolonged periods of high unemployment

3. Prolonged periods of high inflation

4. Simultaneous high inflation and unemployment (stagflation)

9.2 THE CLASSICAL MODEL

The classical model is of old vintage. Aspects of the model form the basis of the beliefs of virtually all economic conservatives.

Say's Law—Named for French economist J. B. Say, the law is frequently expressed as "Supply creates its own demand." What it means is that the process of production generates enough income to buy all the product produced, and, further, there will always be enough spending to buy all the product produced. In other words, a general glut will never occur.

Using the circular flow diagram for a simple pure market economy, assume business produces $5 trillion in goods and services. This means that $5 trillion in incomes (wages, rents, interest, and profits) have been earned by households. Households will spend a portion of that, but will save also. For Say's law to work, business must borrow and use for investment spending the entire amount saved.

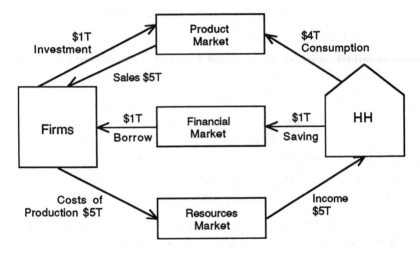

FIGURE 9.1–Circular Flow of Money (Circular Flow of Goods and Services not shown)

Flexible Interest Rates—Flexible interest rates imply that the level of investment will always equal the level of saving. According to the classical economists, the interest rate plays a major role in explaining the levels of both saving and invest-

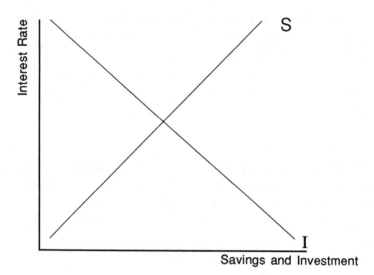

FIGURE 9.2–The Loanable Funds Market

ment. If there is a shortage or surplus of saving, interest rates will adjust to bring saving into equality with investment. Consequently, total spending will always be just adequate to buy all the goods and services produced.

Flexible Wages and Prices—Prolonged unemployment cannot occur as long as wages are flexible. If there are unemployed workers, this must mean that wages are higher than the equilibrium. A drop in wages is all that is needed to bring the economy back to full employment.

While a general glut of goods and services will not occur, there can be shortages and surpluses of specific goods and services. Movements in their prices should be adequate to take care of those problems.

Government Policy—Given the self-regulating nature of the economy, the role of government is inherently limited. In fact, many classical economists blame misguided government policy for many of the more spectacular instances of economic problems. For example, minimum wage laws and government

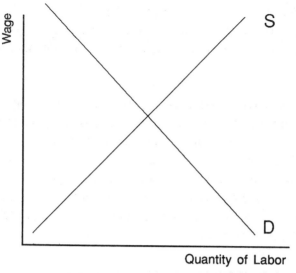

Quantity of Labor

FIGURE 9.3–The Labor Market

support for labor unions have been blamed for reducing wage flexibility. Government attempts to manage interest rates have reduced flexibility here. Government attempts to create money to pay for government programs are often blamed for inflationary problems.

Modern Day Variants—Classical economics as a school of thought cannot be said to exist today. However, classical ideas are promoted by several different schools, the most prominent of which are Monetarism, Rational Expectations, Supply-Side economics, and the Austrian School.

9.3 THE KEYNESIAN MODEL (INCOME-EXPENDITURE MODEL)

John Maynard Keynes and *The General Theory of Employment, Interest and Money* **(1936)**—Keynes (1883-1946, rhymes with "rains") was a British economist who had a distinguished career as a college professor, civil servant, and government advisor. In 1936, during the midst of the world-wide economic depression, he published *The General Theory* as a critique of the classical model and policies. His work was so influential that today most economists consider themselves "Keynesians."

Rigid Downward Wages—Keynes argued that while wages might rise in response to market conditions, they seldom fall. Consequently, unemployment should be considered a normal state of affairs in a capitalistic economy, unless economic policy intervenes. In addition, a general decline in wages during a period of high unemployment would probably not cure the problem because it would mean a general decline in purchasing power. Classical reasoning is an example of a fallacy of composition.

Fallacy of Composition

A fallacy of composition is when you falsely assume what is true for a part is also true for the whole. If you want to see better at a football game you could stand up, but everyone could not see better if everyone stood up.

Instability of Private Investment—Contrary to classical belief, the rate of interest is not a strong determinant of either saving or investment. Saving is more influenced by income and family circumstances. Investment is more influenced by future profit expectations. Consequently, changes in the interest rate cannot be expected to equilibrate saving and investment. In fact, the two magnitudes will seldom be equal because different groups of people make the decisions and there is nothing to coordinate their decisions. In the case of investment, since it is so dependent on future expectations and since expectations are very uncertain and guided by what Keynes called "animal spirits," the level of spending is likely to be highly volatile. Instability will be the hallmark of a capitalistic economy in the absence of appropriate policy.

Paradox of Thrift—To classicals, thriftiness was unambiguously a good thing. Greater saving would automatically lead to greater investment and faster economic growth. To Keynes, greater saving was not always a good thing because there was no guarantee the saving would be converted to investment. If not, the saving would mean less spending which would lead to a contraction of production and unemployment. Thus the paradox was that if everyone tried to save more, they might end up saving less if the economy contracted and incomes fell. This is another example of a fallacy of composition.

Fiscal Policy—Since there was no guarantee that the level of spending would equal the level of production, a role for fiscal policy was created. If government suspects too little spending will be forthcoming, it could increase its own spending or reduce taxes so that the private sector can spend more. If it suspects there will be too much spending, it can do just the opposite with its policy. Thus government's close attention is required if we are to avoid economic instability.

It is accurate to say that Keynes provided a rationale for large-scale government participation in the economy.

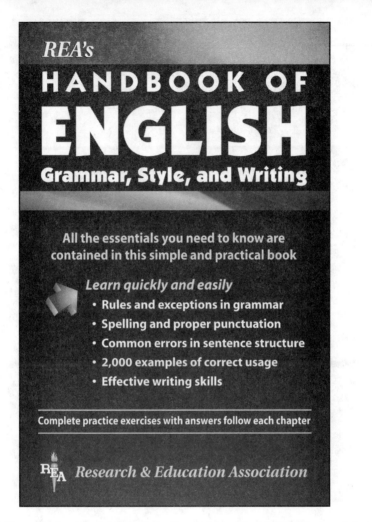

HANDBOOK of
MATHEMATICAL,
SCIENTIFIC, &
ENGINEERING
FORMULAS, FUNCTIONS,
GRAPHS, TABLES,
& TRANSFORMS

R_EA   RESEARCH & EDUCATION ASSOCIATION

A particularly useful reference for those in math, science, engineering and other technical fields. Includes the most-often used formulas, tables, transforms, functions, and graphs which are needed as tools in solving problems. The entire field of special functions is also covered. A large amount of scientific data which is often of interest to scientists and engineers has been included.

Available at your local bookstore or order directly from us by sending in coupon below.

REA's **Problem Solvers**

The "PROBLEM SOLVERS" are comprehensive supplemental text-books designed to save time in finding solutions to problems. Each "PROBLEM SOLVER" is the first of its kind ever produced in its field. It is the product of a massive effort to illustrate almost any imaginable problem in exceptional depth, detail, and clarity. Each problem is worked out in detail with a step-by-step solution, and the problems are arranged in order of complexity from elementary to advanced. Each book is fully indexed for locating problems rapidly.

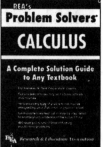

ACCOUNTING	LINEAR ALGEBRA
ADVANCED CALCULUS	MACHINE DESIGN
ALGEBRA & TRIGONOMETRY	MATHEMATICS for ENGINEERS
AUTOMATIC CONTROL	MECHANICS
SYSTEMS/ROBOTICS	NUMERICAL ANALYSIS
BIOLOGY	OPERATIONS RESEARCH
BUSINESS, ACCOUNTING, & FINANCE	OPTICS
CALCULUS	ORGANIC CHEMISTRY
CHEMISTRY	PHYSICAL CHEMISTRY
COMPLEX VARIABLES	PHYSICS
DIFFERENTIAL EQUATIONS	PRE-CALCULUS
ECONOMICS	PROBABILITY
ELECTRICAL MACHINES	PSYCHOLOGY
ELECTRIC CIRCUITS	STATISTICS
ELECTROMAGNETICS	STRENGTH OF MATERIALS &
ELECTRONIC COMMUNICATIONS	MECHANICS OF SOLIDS
ELECTRONICS	TECHNICAL DESIGN GRAPHICS
FINITE & DISCRETE MATH	THERMODYNAMICS
FLUID MECHANICS/DYNAMICS	TOPOLOGY
GENETICS	TRANSPORT PHENOMENA
GEOMETRY	VECTOR ANALYSIS
HEAT TRANSFER	

*If you would like more information about any of these books,
complete the coupon below and return it to us or visit your local bookstore.*

REA's Test Preps
The Best in Test Preparation

- REA "Test Preps" are **far more** comprehensive than any other test preparation series
- Each book contains up to **eight** full-length practice tests based on the most recent exams
- **Every** type of question likely to be given on the exams is included
- Answers are accompanied by **full** and **detailed** explanations

REA publishes over 60 Test Preparation volumes in several series. They include:

Advanced Placement Exams (APs)
Biology
Calculus AB & Calculus BC
Chemistry
Economics
English Language & Composition
English Literature & Composition
European History
Government & Politics
Physics B & C
Psychology
Spanish Language
Statistics
United States History

College-Level Examination Program (CLEP)
Analyzing and Interpreting Literature
College Algebra
Freshman College Composition
General Examinations
General Examinations Review
History of the United States I
History of the United States II
Human Growth and Development
Introductory Sociology
Principles of Marketing
Spanish

SAT Subject Tests
Biology E/M
Chemistry
English Language Proficiency Test
French
German

SAT Subject Tests (cont'd)
Literature
Mathematics Level IC, IIC
Physics
Spanish
United States History
Writing

Graduate Record Exams (GREs)
Biology
Chemistry
Computer Science
General
Literature in English
Mathematics
Physics
Psychology

ACT - ACT Assessment

ASVAB - Armed Services Vocational Aptitude Battery

CBEST - California Basic Educational Skills Test

CDL - Commercial Driver License Exam

CLAST - College Level Academic Skills Test

COOP & HSPT - Catholic High School Admission Tests

ELM - California State University Entry Level Mathematics Exam

FE (EIT) - Fundamentals of Engineering Exams - For both AM & PM Exams

FTCE - Florida Teacher Certification Exam

GED - High School Equivalency Diploma Exam (U.S. & Canadian editions)

GMAT CAT - Graduate Management Admission Test

LSAT - Law School Admission Test

MAT - Miller Analogies Test

MCAT - Medical College Admission Test

MTEL - Massachusetts Tests for Educator Licensure

MSAT - Multiple Subjects Assessment for Teachers

NJ HSPA - New Jersey High School Proficiency Assessment

NYSTCE: LAST & ATS-W - New York State Teacher Certification

PLT - Principles of Learning & Teaching Tests

PPST - Pre-Professional Skills Tests

PSAT - Preliminary Scholastic Assessment Test

SAT

TExES - Texas Examinations of Educator Standards

THEA - Texas Higher Education Assessment

TOEFL - Test of English as a Foreign Language

TOEIC - Test of English for International Communication

USMLE Steps 1,2,3 - U.S. Medical Licensing Exams

U.S. Postal Exams 460 & 470

RESEARCH & EDUCATION ASSOCIATION
61 Ethel Road W. • Piscataway, New Jersey 08854
Phone: (732) 819-8880   website: www.rea.com

Please send me more information about your Test Prep books

Name _____

Address _____

City _____ State _____ Zip _____